3-D TEACHING AIDS

by
Lynn Brisson

Incentive Publications, Inc.
Nashville, Tennessee

Illustrated by Lynn Brisson
Cover by Susan Eaddy
Edited by Sally Sharpe

ISBN 0-86530-072-0

Table of Contents

COMPLETE, ILLUSTRATED INSTRUCTIONS FOR USING THIS BOOK

3-D TEACHING AIDS provides you with a variety of creative and easy-to-make projects that can be utilized as art activities as well as valuable teaching tools. These 3-D creations can be made by the students themselves and can be used for individual or group learning activities, bulletin boards and displays, communicators and awards, and much more. To help you get the most use out of this book, this introduction has been designed to give you as many helpful suggestions and ideas for using the materials in this book as possible. Refer to it again and again to spark your own creative ideas.

The projects found on pages 9 - 44 follow the same procedural format. Each project provides you with a listing of necessary materials, step-by-step construction directions, and ideas for specific uses. In addition to the suggested uses, you will think of countless other ways to use the patterns and projects to meet the unique needs and capabilities of your students. All of the patterns can be adapted for use in bulletin board displays. Give the students the creative freedom to formulate their own ideas for other uses, too.

The projects found on pages 45 - 63 have been designed to be used as 3-D work sheets. Each project provides you with step-by-step construction directions and suggestions for additional uses. All of the work sheet projects require the following materials: construction paper, crayons or colored pencils, scissors, and glue, paper clips or staples (to use in attaching the stand-up characters to the work sheets). According to your particular situation and needs, you may choose to follow one or more of the procedures described below:

1. Allow the students to construct the work sheets. Have the students copy the activity onto their work sheets from the board or some other source.
2. Allow the students to construct the work sheets. Collect the work sheets and prepare the activity. Redistribute the work sheets and have the students complete the activity.
3. Construct the work sheets and prepare the activity. Distribute the work sheets and have the students complete the activity.
4. Give the students prepared activities on "flat" work sheets (work sheets without the stand-up characters). After reviewing or grading each activity, write your comments or the student's grade on the stand-up character. Attach the characters to the work sheets and distribute them to the students.
5. Allow the students to construct the work sheets and to use them in other ways as suggested by the individual projects.

Activities of every kind and every subject or theme can be used with the work sheets. The possibilities are endless. Choose puzzles; mazes; fill-in-the-blank, multiple choice, completion, matching, and question-and-answer activities for math, science, social studies, health, grammar, reading, writing, and other subjects. The examples below may give you a few ideas.

NAME

Write a story about what could happen if you found a dinosaur's egg in your back yard.

NAME

Take a sensory scavenger hunt around the classroom.
Look for an item which fits each description below.
1. something nice to look at _____
2. something cold to touch _____
3. something bright to see _____
4. something impossible to smell _____

5. something unpleasant to taste _____

NAME

Write the definition for each word below and then use the word in a sentence.
1. definite

2. careful

3. exact

NAME

Circle the words that describe emotions or feelings.

S	i	l	l	y	o
h	a	p	p	y	e
y	n	r	s	f	t
b	g	o	a	d	i
r	r	u	d	n	c
e	y	d	g	s	a

NAME

Complete the multiplication and division problems below.

6
x6   12
x3   21
x6   20)400   5)64   4)125

All of the 3-D work sheets lend themselves to many other uses. In addition to the specific suggestions given with each project, the ideas below may be used with the work sheets to extend their use in and out of the classroom.

- messages to parents

- homework assignments
- tests
- board work
- learning center activities
- school announcements

- party and open house invitations
- name markers to identify students' desks and/or work areas

- place mats
  (Hint: Enlarge and laminate the patterns.)

- puppets
  (Hint: Cut the tabs off of the characters and glue craft sticks to the backs of the characters. Use the work sheets for scenery.)

- matching games
  (Hint: Write a question on each work sheet and the answer on the "corresponding" character. Let the students match the questions and answers.)

- awards

- displays
  (Hint: Display leaves, insects, rocks, and other "collections" on the work sheets.)

- bulletin boards
  (Hint: Enlarge the patterns if desired.)

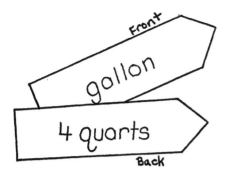

STEGOSAURUS STUDY BUDDY

Materials:
- construction paper
- crayons or colored pencils
- scissors
- glue

Construction:
1. Cut the Stegosaurus and "spike" patterns out of construction paper. Fold the Stegosaurus pattern along the dotted lines.
2. Place a strip of glue on each side of the Stegosaurus (on the inside), but not across the top. Press the sides together to form a pocket.
3. Color the Stegosaurus with crayons or colored pencils.

Uses:
- Have the students write on the "spikes" information that they can study or "drill" individually on in pairs. Students may write one piece of information on one side of each "spike" and the corresponding information on the other side. The students may store the "spikes" in the pocket.
- Instruct the students to write a dinosaur name on one side of each "spike" and information about that dinosaur on the other side.
- Write questions on the "spikes" and have the students write the answers on the backs of the "spikes."

9

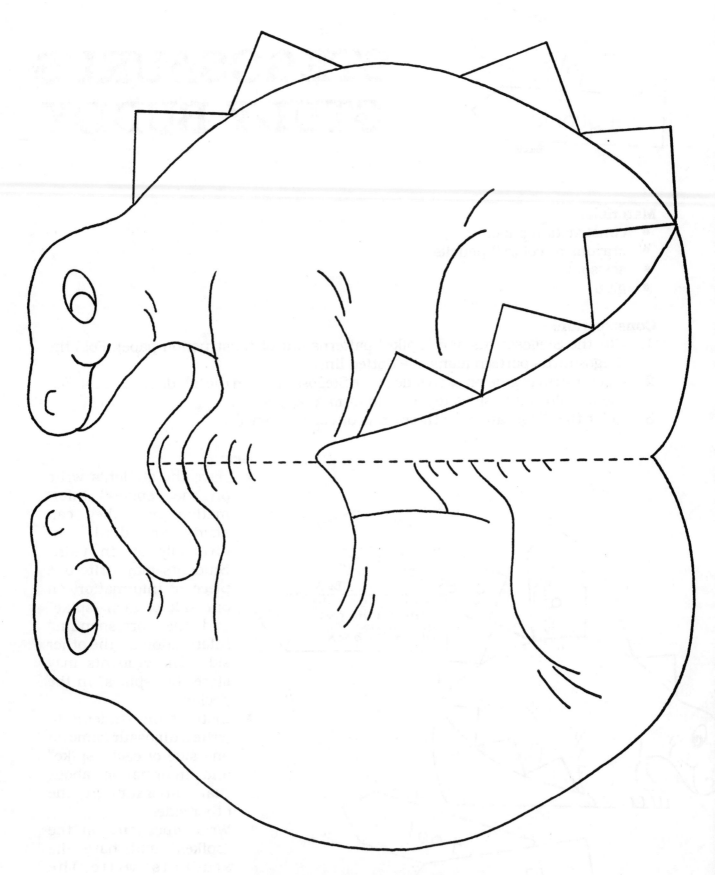

Fold along the dotted lines.

PROUD PEACOCK

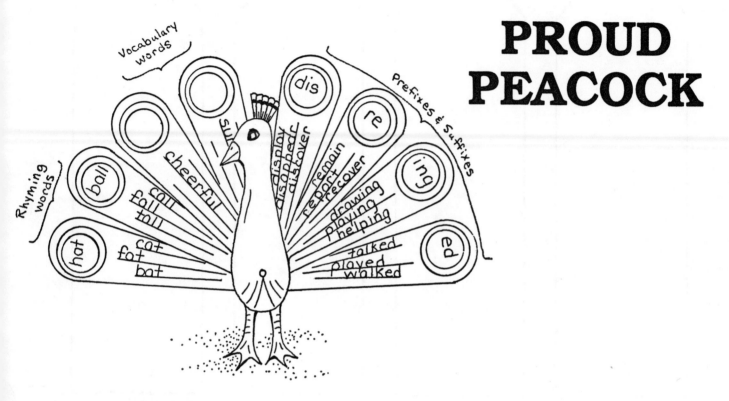

Materials:
- construction paper
- crayons or colored pencils
- scissors
- brads

Construction:
1. Cut the peacock pattern and eight feather patterns out of construction paper.
2. Color the peacock's body and tail feathers with crayons or colored pencils.
3. Use a brad to attach the feathers to the peacock body and then "fan" the feathers.

Uses:
- Have the students write rhyming words, vocabulary words, prefixes, suffixes, and other kinds of "information" to be studied on the tail feathers.
- Write a story starter on each feather and pin the peacock to a bulletin board. Ask each student to select a story starter and to complete the story. Display the stories on the bulletin board.
- Ask each student to write his or her name on a peacock and one word that describes his or her personality on each feather.

Cut 8 feathers.

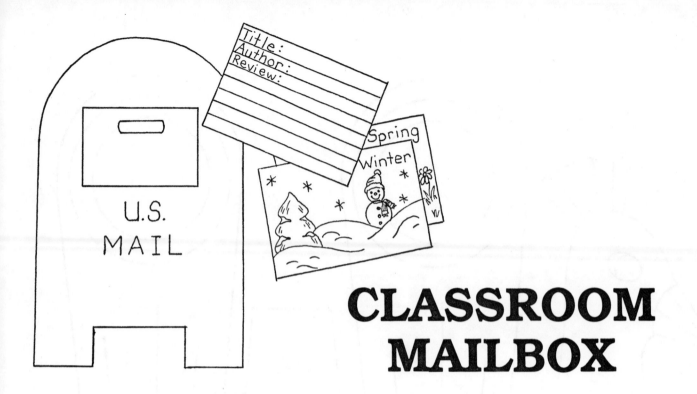

CLASSROOM MAILBOX

Materials:
- construction paper
- crayons or colored pencils
- scissors
- glue
- 3" x 5" cards

Construction:
1. Cut two mailbox patterns (one with a "door" and one without) out of construction paper. Color the patterns.
2. Cut the "door" along the dotted lines.
3. Place a strip of glue around the outer edges of both patterns (on the "inside") and glue the patterns together.

Uses:
- Write "information" for the students to study or "drill" on the cards and store the cards inside the mailbox.
- Have the students write letters to real or imaginary people and "mail" their letters.
- Instruct the students to cut pictures representative of foreign countries out of magazines and paste them on cards. Have the students write "post card greetings" on the backs of the cards and "mail" their cards.
- Have the students write book reviews on the cards.

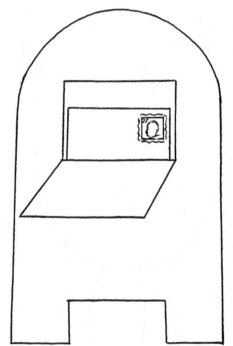

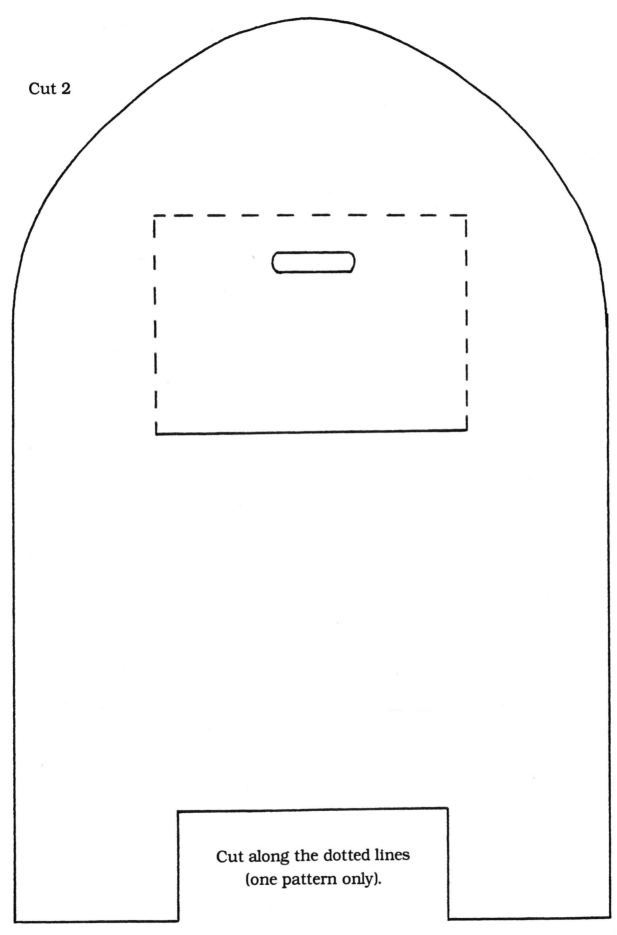

Cut 2

Cut along the dotted lines
(one pattern only).

POCKET CAMERA

Materials:
- construction paper
- crayons or colored pencils
- yarn
- hole punch
- scissors
- glue
- 3" x 5" cards

Construction:
1. Cut the camera pattern out of construction paper. Fold the pattern along the dotted lines.
2. Place a strip of glue on each side of the camera (on the inside), but not across the top. Press the sides together to form a pocket.
3. Color the camera with crayons or colored pencils.
4. Punch a hole at the top of each side of the camera and tie yarn through each hole to make a hanging loop.

Uses:
- Let the students draw pictures on their cards relating to stories they are reading, lessons they are studying, etc. Or, have the students cut pictures out of magazines to paste on their cards. Students will enjoy placing their cards in their cameras and wearing them around their necks!
- Ask each student to write about his or her family on one side of a card and to draw a picture of the family on the other side. Instruct the students to place their family photographs in their cameras.

Fold along the dotted lines.

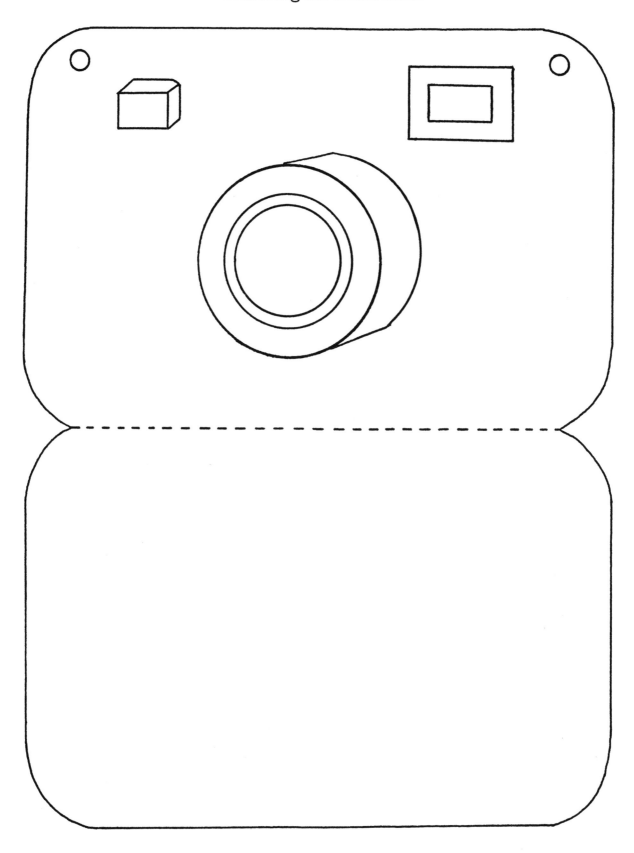

POCKET PEARLS

Materials:
- construction paper
- crayons or colored pencils
- scissors
- glue

Construction:
1. Cut the shell and pearl patterns out of construction paper. Fold the shell pattern along the dotted lines.
2. Place a strip of glue on each side of the shell (on the inside), but not across the top. Press the sides together to form a pocket.
3. Color the shell with crayons or colored pencils.

Uses:
- Have the students write on the pearls information that they can study or "drill" individually or in pairs. Students may write one piece of information on one side of each pearl and the corresponding information on the other side.
- Use the patterns to create an attractive and informative bulletin board about "life under the sea."

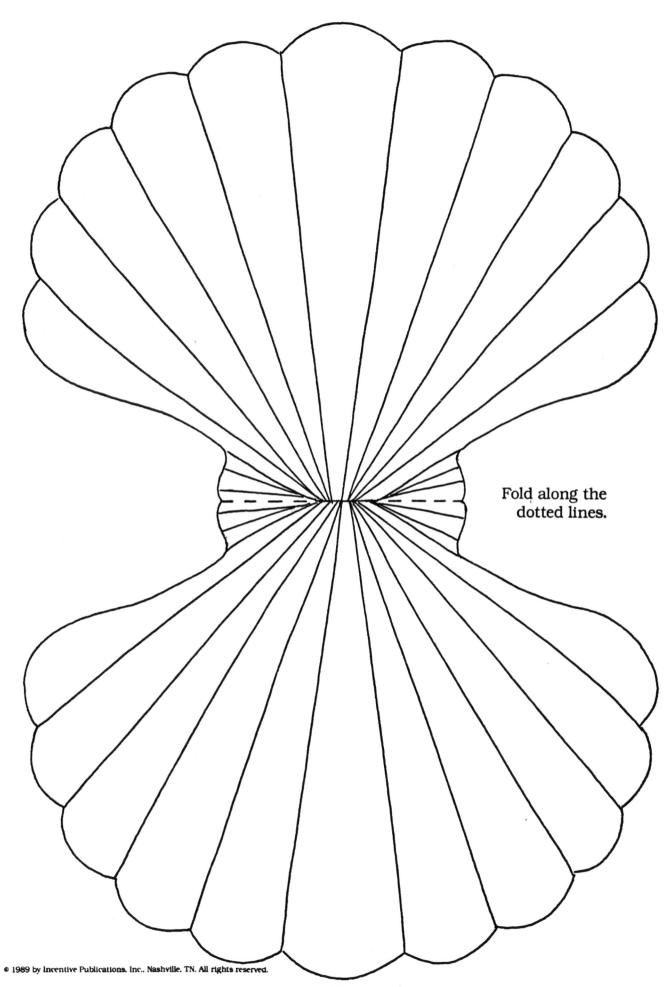

Fold along the
dotted lines.

A POPPING GOOD TIME!

Materials:
- construction paper
- crayons or colored pencils
- scissors
- glue

Construction:
1. Cut the popcorn and popcorn box patterns out of construction paper.
2. Fold the popcorn box along the dotted lines.
3. Place a strip of glue on each side of the popcorn box (on the inside), but not across the top. Press the sides together to form a pocket.
4. Color the popcorn box with crayons or colored pencils.
5. Glue some popcorn pieces inside the popcorn box.

Uses:
- Write "information" for the students to study, "drill," or review on the popcorn pieces (i.e. days of the week, numbers, letters, etc.). Store the popcorn in the box.
- Write the numbers 1-31 on popcorn pieces and place them inside the popcorn box. Attach the box to a bulletin board next to a large calendar. Each day, let a student remove the correct number and attach it to the calendar.
- Place the popcorn box in a learning center or free-time area and let the students use the popcorn pieces as game markers.
- Enlarge the patterns. Write each student's name on a popcorn pattern and use the popcorn pieces as name tags. Attach the popcorn box to the classroom door or a bulletin board.

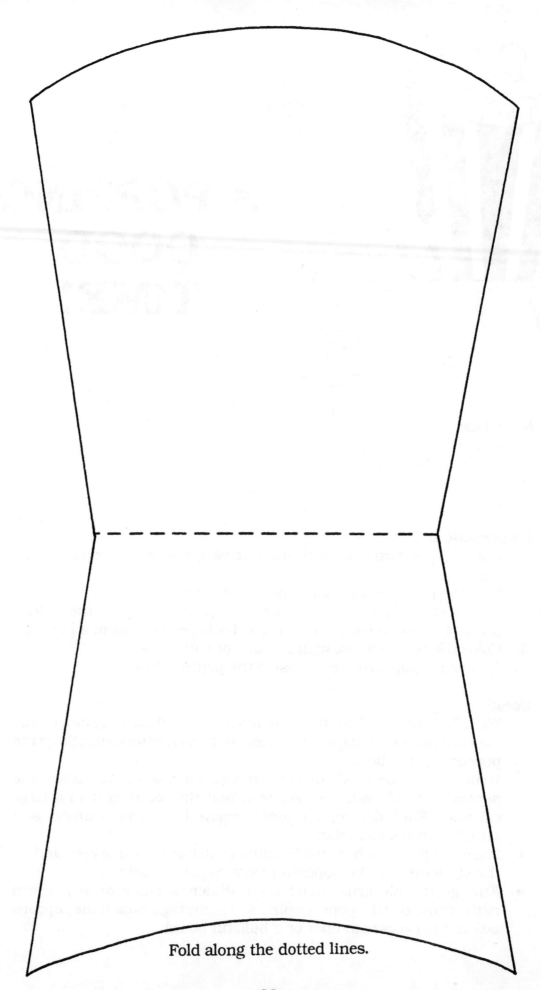

Fold along the dotted lines.

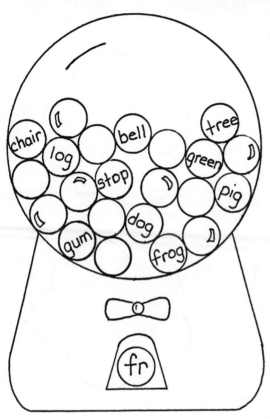

3-D GUMBALL MACHINE

Materials:
- construction paper
- crayons or colored pencils
- scissors
- glue
- brads

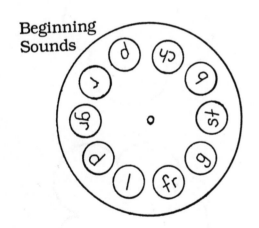

Beginning Sounds

Construction:
1. Cut all of the patterns out of construction paper.
2. Cut the gumball machine along the dotted lines. Fold the cut edges over to the lines indicated and glue in place.
3. Write the information to be taught or reinforced on the wheel (i.e. beginning sounds, numbers, math problems, etc.).
4. Insert a brad through the knob pattern and then through the gumball machine and wheel patterns respectively.
5. Color the gumballs and the gumball machine if desired.

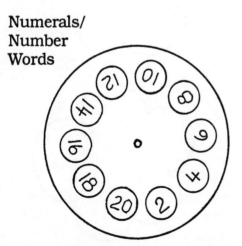

Numerals/
Number
Words

Uses:
- Instruct each student to turn the wheel to a gumball and to write the corresponding information or "answer" on one of the gumballs "inside" the machine.
- Attach the gumball machine to a bulletin board display and let the students go to the board in their free time to complete the activity.

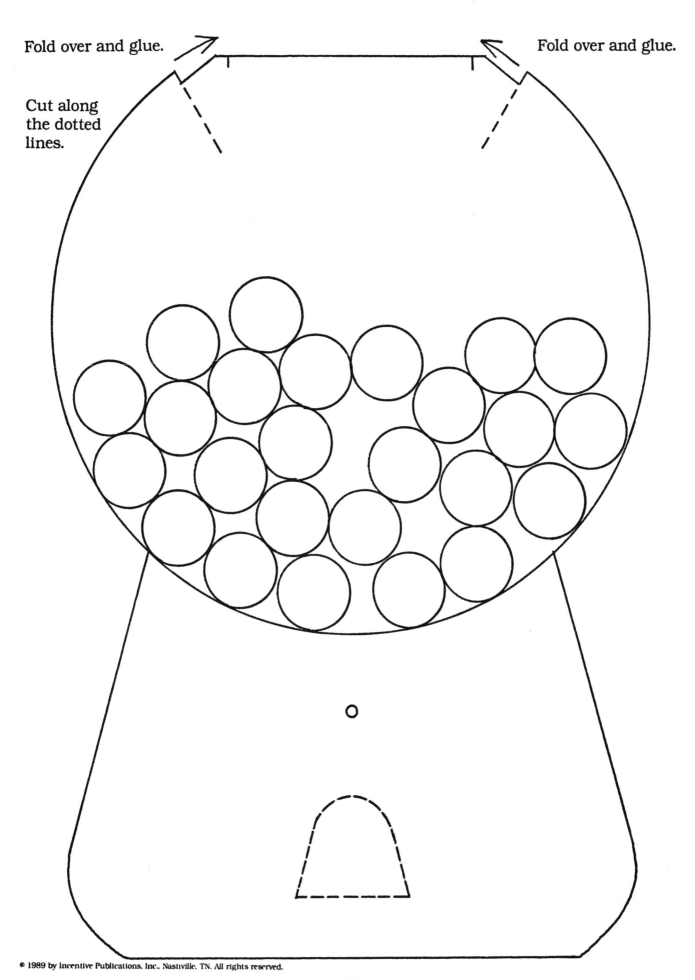

Fold over and glue.

Fold over and glue.

Cut along the dotted lines.

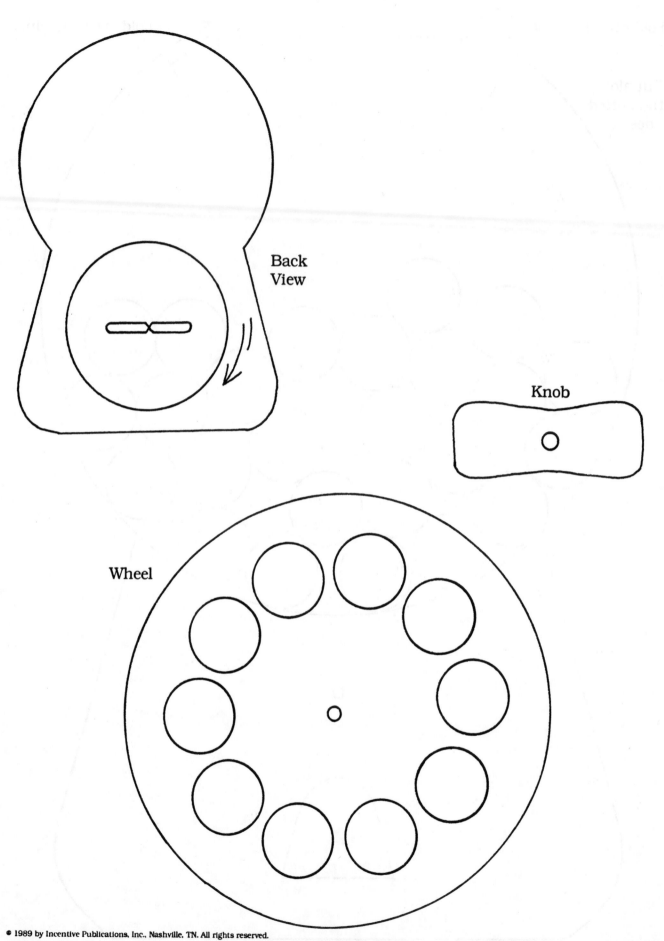

Back View

Knob

Wheel

SEA SCENE

Materials:
- construction paper
- crayons or markers
- scissors
- glue
- sand or salt (optional)

Construction:
1. Cut the patterns out of construction paper. Cut each pattern along the dotted lines.
2. Insert the seaweed patterns into the slits in the background pattern to make a stand-up background.
3. (Optional) Spread glue on the bottom of the background pattern and sprinkle sand or salt over the glue.
4. Draw an ocean scene on the stand-up background.

Uses:
- Have the students write reports or facts about ocean life on the backs of their stand-up scenes.
- Ask the students to write "sea stories" on the backs of their sea pictures.
- Use the completed scenes as "backdrops" for science displays, reports, experiments, etc.

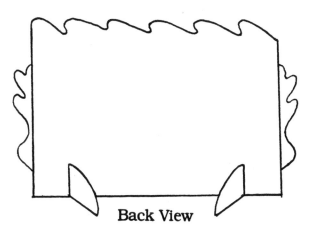

Back View

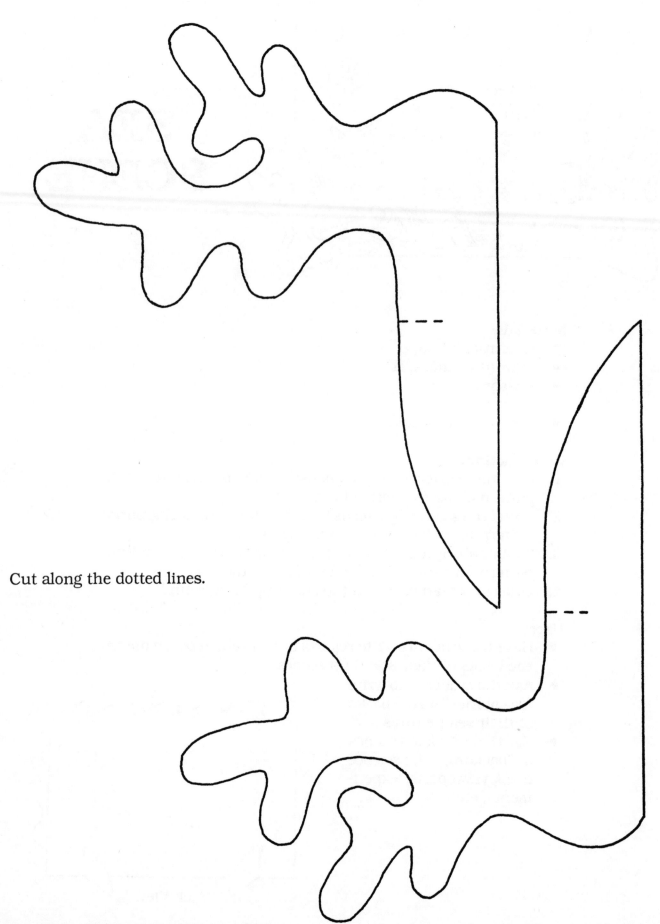

Cut along the dotted lines.

Cut along the dotted lines.

STAND-UP CERTIFICATE

Materials:
- construction paper
- crayons or markers
- scissors

Construction:
1. Cut the certificate out of construction paper and write the appropriate information on the certificate with a pen or marker.
2. Decorate the certificate with crayons or markers or allow the student to do this at a later time.
3. Cut the certificate along the dotted lines and then fold back the tabs to make it stand up.

Uses:
- Create many different kinds of certificates simply by changing the information on the certificate.
- Let the students make certificates for each other.
- Use the stand-up certificate pattern to make invitations or greeting cards.
- Write instructions for learning center activities on stand-up certificates.
- Have the students write stories or poems on certificates for display in a reading corner.
- Write book reports or summaries on certificates to be displayed "behind" the books in a reading center.
- Display students' work on stand-up certificates.

Back View

Cut along the dotted lines and fold back the tabs.

STAND-UP SNOWMAN

Materials
- construction paper
- scissors
- glue
- cotton balls
- silver glitter
- small paper plates
- crayons or colored pencils

Construction:
1. Cut the snowman pattern out of construction paper and color the snowman's hat, eyes, nose, buttons and mittens with crayons or colored pencils.
2. Spread a thin sheet of glue over the uncolored parts of the snowman and sprinkle silver glitter over the glue.
3. Fold back the tab on the snowman, place glue on the tab, and attach the snowman to a small paper plate.
4. Glue cotton balls to the paper plate to cover it.

Uses:
- Group the students' snowmen to create an attractive display.
- Let the students take their snowmen home for use as table centerpieces or room decorations.
- To make a 3-D snowman work sheet, simply glue the snowman to a sheet of construction paper which has been trimmed into an oval shape.

Back View

Tab

HEART BASKET

Materials:
- construction paper
- hole punch
- yarn or ribbon
- crayons or markers
- scissors
- glue

Construction:
1. Cut the heart basket pattern out of construction paper.
2. Decorate the basket with crayons or markers.
3. Fold the basket along the dotted lines and glue the tab to the inside of the opposite heart.
4. Punch a hole in each heart. Run yarn or ribbon through the holes to make a hanging loop and secure the loop by tying a bow.

Uses:
- Students will enjoy making heart baskets for Christmas, Valentine's Day, and other special occasions.
- Let each student make a heart basket to hold valentines from classmates. Hang the baskets on the students' desks or display them on a bulletin board.
- Have the students fill the baskets with goodies and give them to special people as gifts.
- Fill heart baskets with special treats and give them to the students as party favors (parents may be willing to help!).

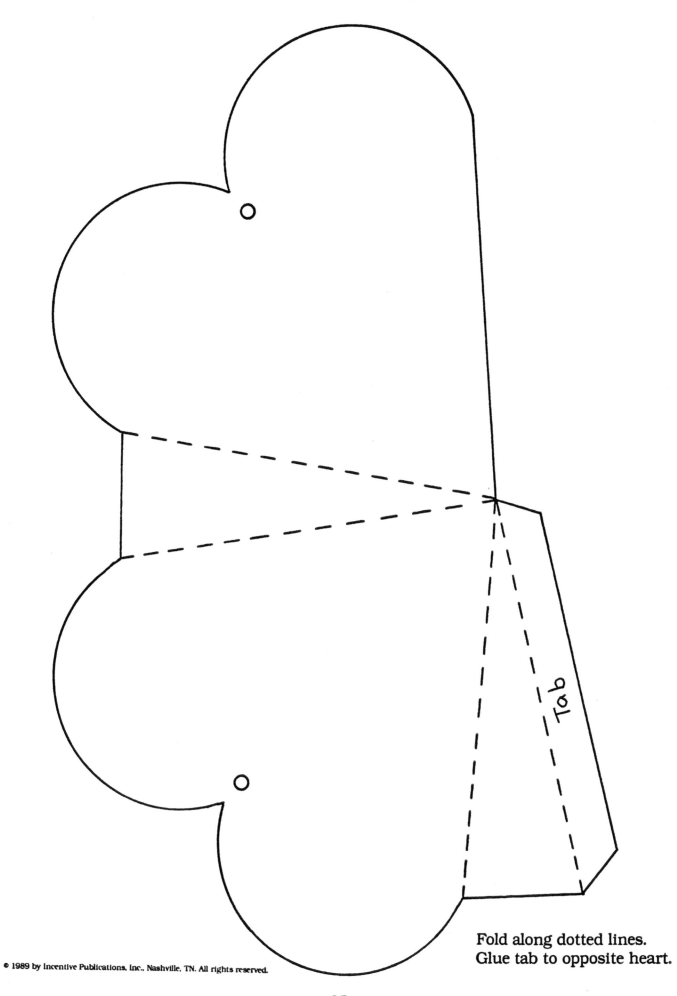

Fold along dotted lines.
Glue tab to opposite heart.

Tab

GIFT CARD

Materials:
- construction paper
- scissors
- glue
- crayons or markers
- packages of flower seeds

Construction:
1. Cut the basket out of construction paper. Cut along the dotted lines to make a handle (folding the pattern makes this easier).
2. Fold a 9" x 12" piece of construction paper in half.
3. Place the basket pattern in the center of the folded paper and trace around the inside of the basket handle. Cut out the traced area.
4. Glue the basket to the folded card and tape or glue the package of flower seeds inside the card. (Be sure that the flowers on the package can be seen through the opening.)
5. Decorate the front and inside of the card using crayons or markers. Add a special message.

Uses:
- Students will enjoy making gift cards for many different occasions: birthdays, Valentine's Day, Mother's Day, Father's Day, Christmas, etc.

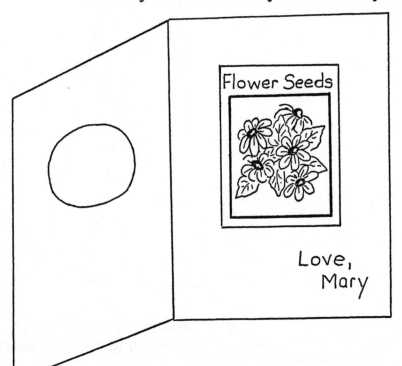

- Instead of using flower seed packages, have the students draw their own flowers or glue pictures of flowers or construction paper flowers inside their cards.
- To make an Easter card, instruct the students to draw colorful eggs or glue construction paper eggs inside their baskets.

Cut along the dotted lines.

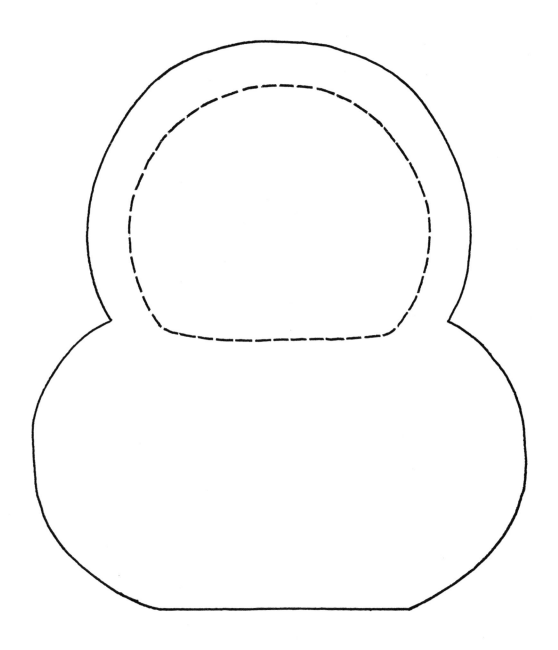

PAPER BAG RABBIT

Materials:

- construction paper
- scissors
- glue
- crayons or markers
- paper lunch bags
- artificial grass (optional)

Construction:

1. Cut the patterns out of construction paper.
2. Place the rabbit pattern on a flattened bag and cut around the pattern as instructed by the diagram below (DO NOT cut below the arrows).
3. Glue construction paper arms to the sides of the bag.
4. Use crayons or markers to add features to the rabbit, or cut the features out of construction paper and glue them to the bag.

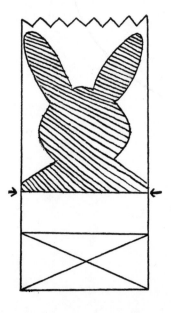

Cut around the pattern to the arrows. DO NOT cut below the arrows.

Uses:

- Write "information" for the students to study or "drill" on the carrots. Place the carrots in the rabbit bag and have the students write the correct information or "answers" on the backs of the carrots.
- Have each student make a rabbit bag to use as an Easter treat bag. Fill the bags with artificial grass or construction paper grass and let the students hunt for eggs in the classroom or a designated area outside.

Fold

Cut two

Glue

Fold over

FRIENDLY BOOKMARKS

Materials:
- construction paper
- crayons or markers
- scissors

Construction:
1. Cut the bookmarks out of construction paper.
2. Add details to the bookmarks with crayons or markers.

Uses:
- Instruct the students to write the title of the book, the author's name, and any new words they learn on a bookmark. Have the students look up the words in a dictionary and write the definitions on another piece of paper.
- Students may use the bookmarks as reading records by writing the titles of the books they read on the bookmarks.
- Have each student make a bookmark for each subject and record all homework assignments on the bookmarks.

Books I've Read

The Sleeping Beauty

Mouse Tales

Max Flies His Kite

Seven Little Rabbits

The Very Hungry Caterpillar

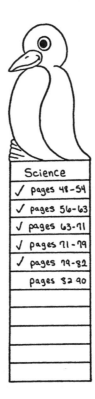

Science

✓ pages 48-54

✓ pages 56-63

✓ pages 63-71

✓ pages 71-79

✓ pages 79-82

pages 82-90

Title: Possum Magic

Author: Mem Fox

New Words:

Vegemite

invisible

wombat

shrink

Mornay

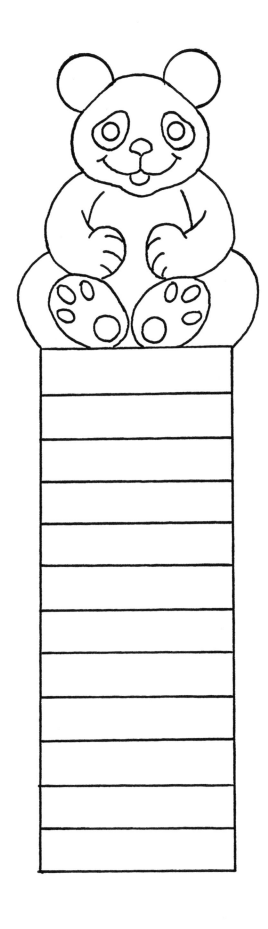
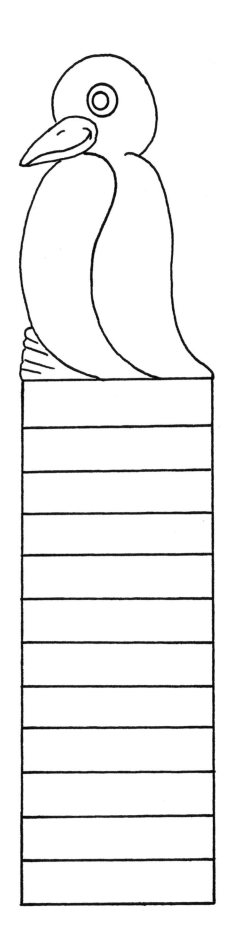

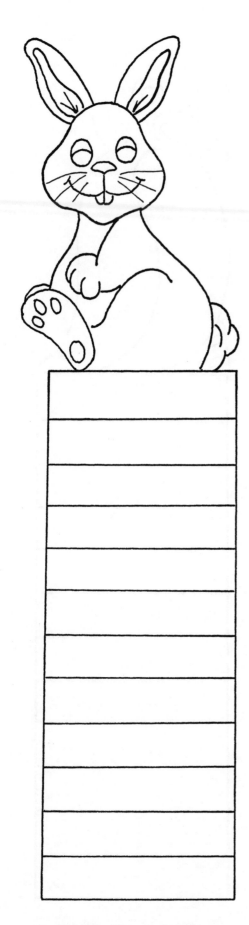

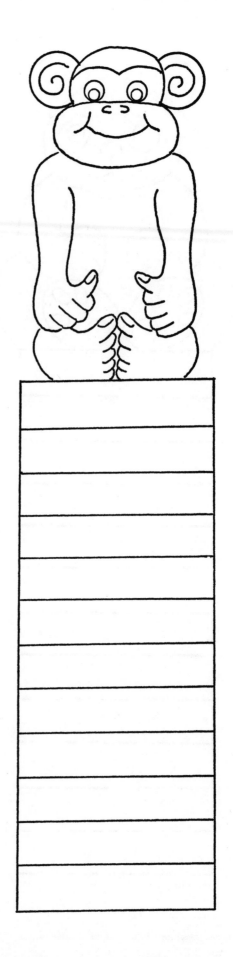

UPSIDE-DOWN CLOWN

Construction:

1. Cut the clown pattern out of construction paper.
2. Cut a large circle out of construction paper (approximately 7 inches in diameter), write "name" at the top of the circle, and draw a blank for the student's name.
3. Prepare the activity or instruct the students to do so.
4. After completing the activity, the students may color the clown and circle patterns.
5. Instruct each student to fold back the tab and attach the clown to the circle using glue, paper clips or staples.

Suggestions:

Refer to pages 6 - 8 for general subject matter and classroom use suggestions.

- Use upside-down clown as a poster on which to write classroom rules, assignments, the weekly spelling list, etc.
- Enlarge the patterns to make a birthday poster on which to announce students' birthdays. Let the students make 3-D birthday cards with original messages.
- Use upside-down clown to make fun five-minute filler activities such as word puzzles, mazes, brain teasers, etc.

Tab

DYNAMIC DINOSAUR

Construction:

1. Cut the patterns out of construction paper.
2. Prepare the activity or instruct the students to do so.
3. After completing the activity, the students may color the egg and dinosaur patterns.
4. Instruct each student to fold back the tab and attach the dinosaur to the egg using glue, paper clips or staples.

Suggestions:

Refer to pages 6 - 8 for general subject matter and classroom use suggestions.

- Instruct the students to write creative stories about "the day the baby dinosaur was hatched."
- Have the students prepare fact sheets for specific dinosaurs.
- Let the students create their own "prehistoric" word find and crossword puzzles.

Tab

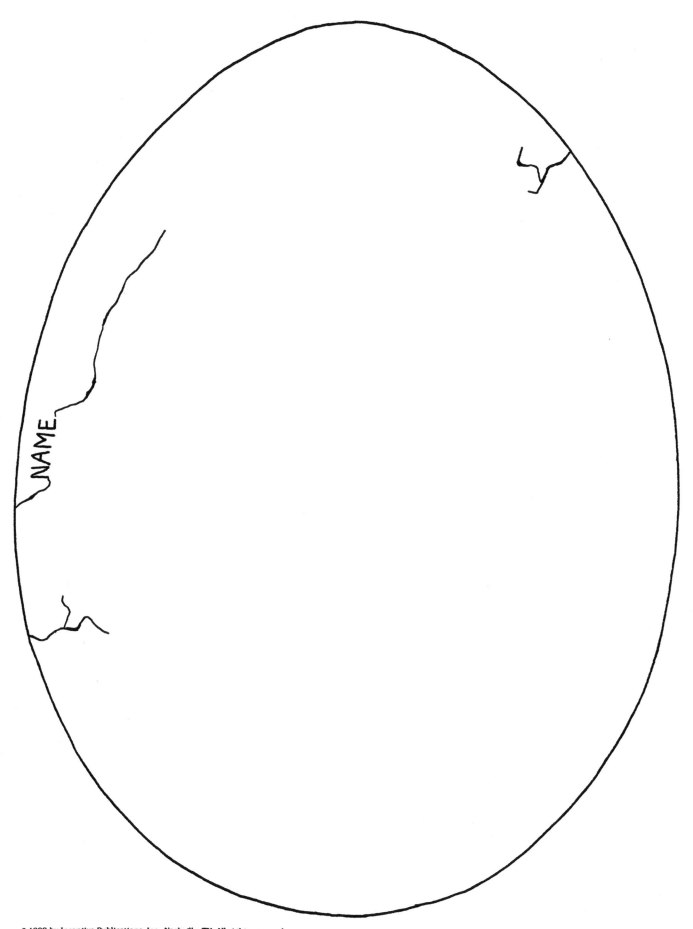

NAME

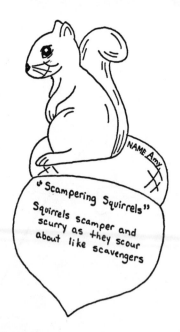

SCAMPERING SQUIRREL

Construction:

1. Cut the patterns out of construction paper.
2. Prepare the activity or instruct the students to do so.
3. After completing the activity, the students may color the acorn and squirrel patterns.
4. Instruct each student to fold back the tab and attach the squirrel to the acorn using glue, paper clips or staples.

Suggestions:

Refer to pages 6 - 8 for general subject matter and classroom use suggestions.

- Have the students mount and label on their work sheets various kinds of nuts.
- Ask each student to write a brief report about an animal that gathers food for the winter.
- Discuss alliteration. Have the students write alliterative poems about squirrels.

Tab

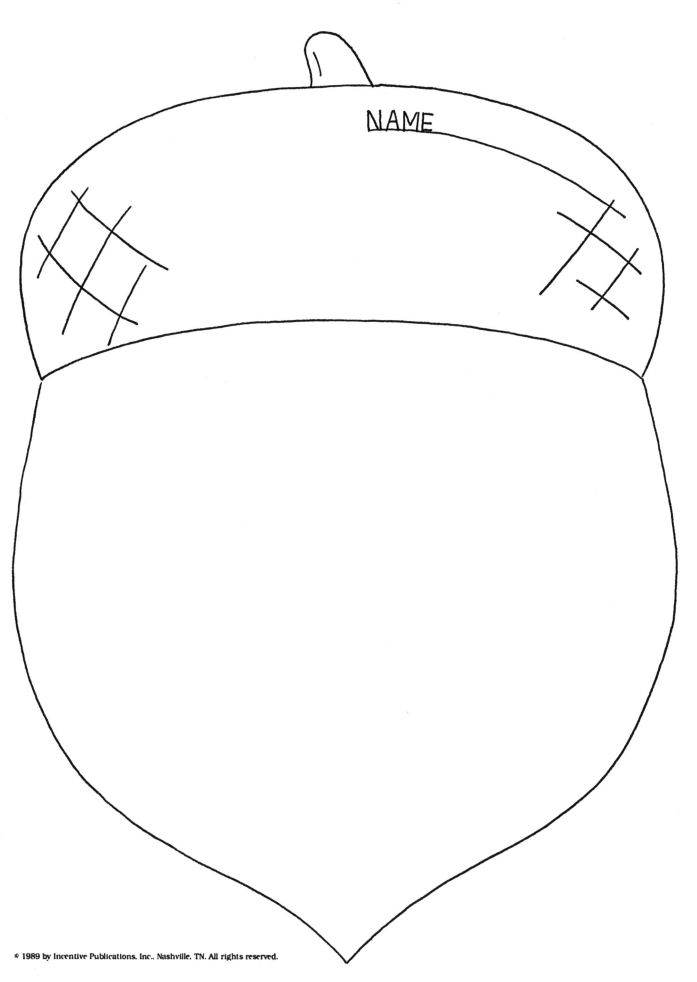

NAME

"BATTY" JACK-O'-LANTERN

Construction:
1. Cut the patterns out of construction paper.
2. Prepare the activity or instruct the students to do so.
3. After completing the activity, the students may color the jack-o'-lantern and bat patterns.
4. Instruct each student to fold back the tab and attach the bat to the jack-o'-lantern using glue, paper clips or staples.

Suggestions:
Refer to pages 6 - 8 for general subject matter and classroom use suggestions.

- Have the students write spooky Halloween tales on the jack-o'-lanterns.
- Use the jack-o'-lanterns as booklet covers for the students' work.
- Laminate the patterns to make 3-D place mats for a class Halloween party.
- Use the work sheets to give everyday math, science, and other subject activities "seasonal" excitement.

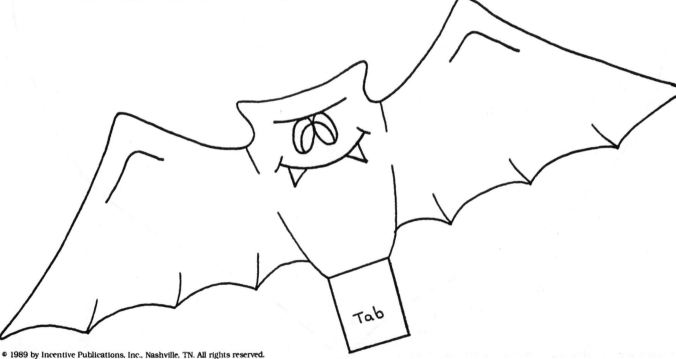

NAME

Cool Penguin Says...

1. Eat balanced meals with foods from the four food groups.
2. Brush your teeth after eating.
3. Exercise regulary.
4. Wash with soap and water every day.

NAME

COOL PENGUIN

Tab

Construction:

1. Cut the patterns out of construction paper.
2. Prepare the activity or instruct the students to do so.
3. After completing the activity, the students may color the penguin and ice block patterns.
4. Instruct each student to fold back the tab and attach the penguin to the ice block using glue, paper clips or staples.

Suggestions:

Refer to pages 6 - 8 for general subject matter and classroom use suggestions.

- Discuss good grooming and health habits. Have the students write grooming and health tips and "rules" on the ice blocks.
- Have the students write reports about countries with very cold climates and the animals that inhabit those countries.

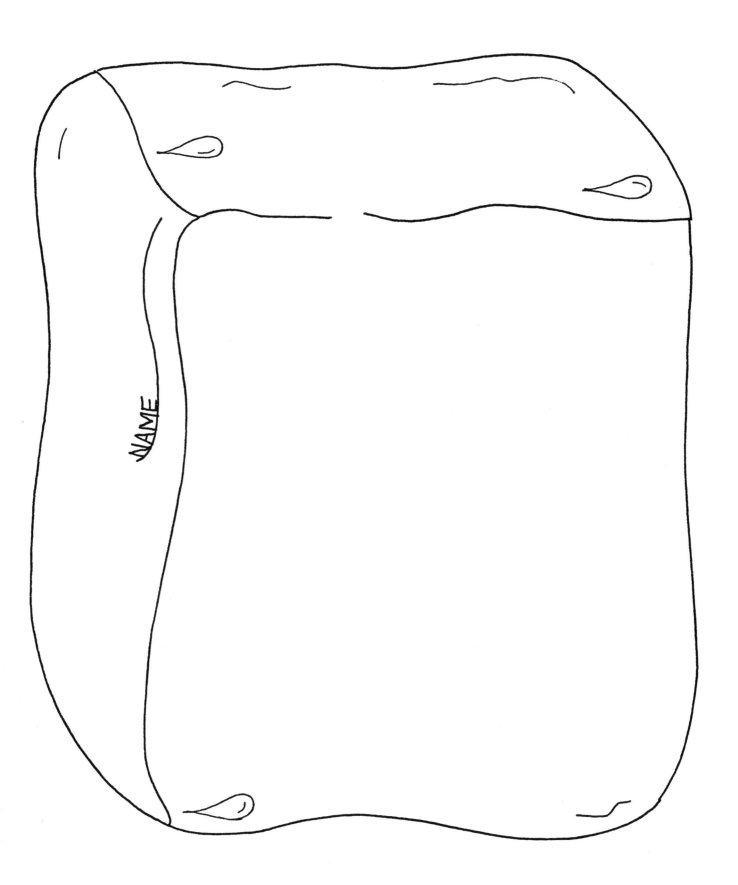

NAME

MERRY MOUSE

Construction:

1. Cut the patterns out of construction paper.
2. Prepare the activity or instruct the students to do so.
3. After completing the activity, the students may color the mouse and cheese patterns.
4. Instruct each student to fold back the tab and attach the mouse to the cheese using glue, paper clips or staples.

Suggestions:

Refer to pages 6 - 8 for general subject matter and classroom use suggestions.

- Create a "Big Cheese Award" for students who excel or improve in certain areas.
- Have the students write "mini-adventures."
- Write a bibliography of good books to read on the cheese and place Merry Mouse in a reading corner.

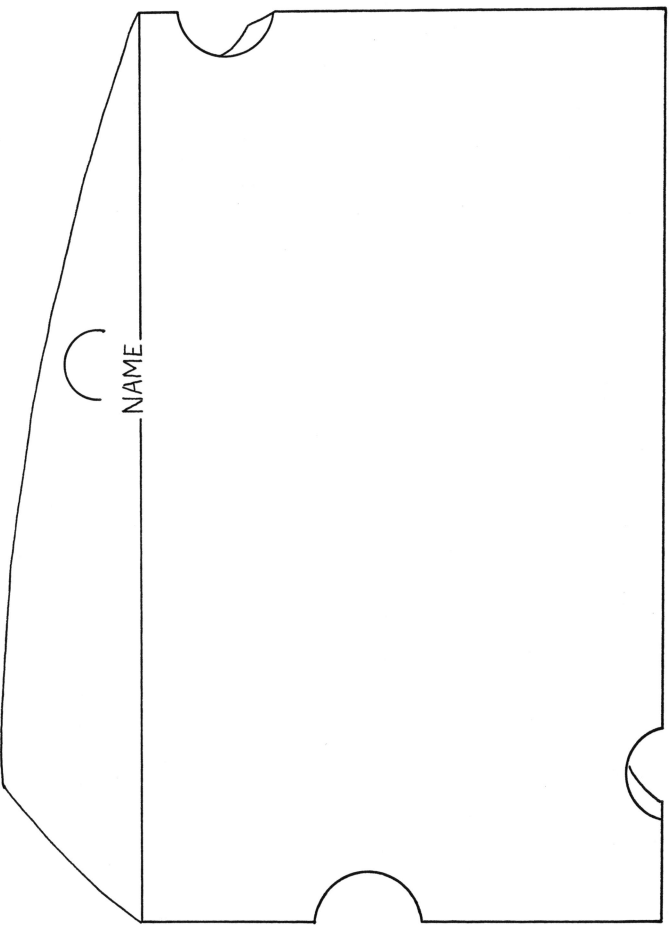

NAME

To a "Bear-y" Nice
Teacher.
Happy Valentine's Day!
Love,
Ginny

NAME Ms. Thomas

BASHFUL BEAR

Tab

Construction:

1. Cut the patterns out of construction paper.
2. Prepare the activity or instruct the students to do so.
3. After completing the activity, the students may color the bear and heart patterns.
4. Instruct each student to fold back the tab and attach the bear to the heart using glue, paper clips or staples.

Suggestions:

Refer to pages 6 - 8 for general subject matter and classroom use suggestions.

- Write this heading on each work sheet: The "Bear" Facts About _____."
  Have the students write reports about suggested topics.
- Let the students write original Valentine's Day messages on these 3-D valentines to deliver to classmates and the school's staff.

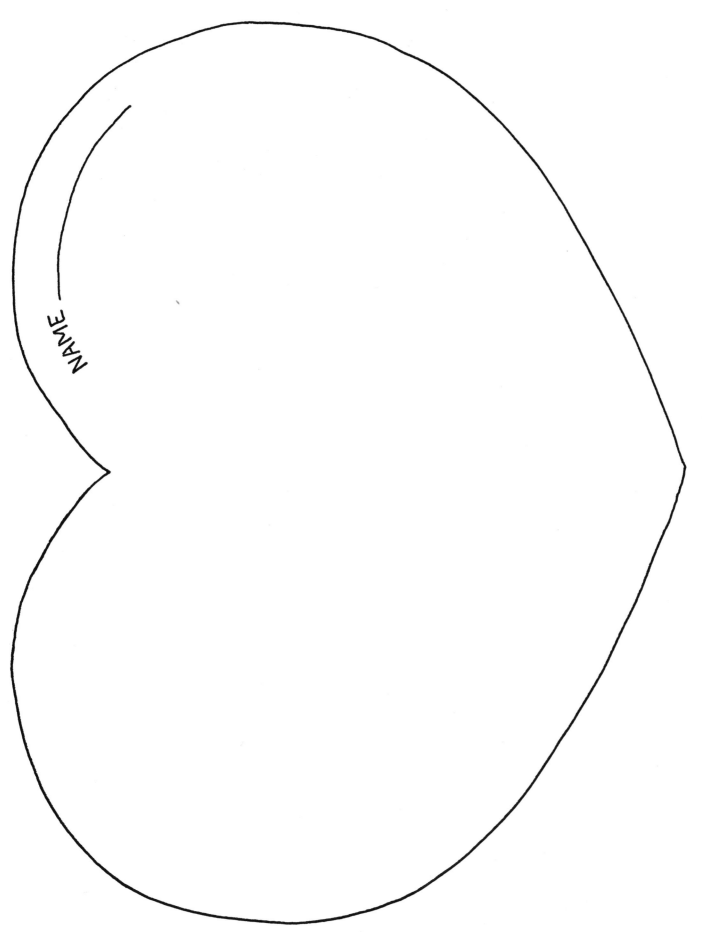

NAME

This "Shiny Apple"
is presented to

Susan

for
good behavior!

Mrs. Applebee
signed

WIGGLY WORM

Construction:
1. Cut the patterns out of construction paper.
2. Prepare the activity or instruct the students to do so.
3. After completing the activity, the students may color the apple and worm patterns.
4. Instruct each student to fold back the tab and attach the worm to the apple using glue, paper clips or staples.

Suggestions:
Refer to pages 6 - 8 for general subject matter and classroom use suggestions.

- Have the students write brief autobiographies for a "first of school" activity. Arrange an attractive tabletop display or create a "flat" bulletin board display by cutting a slit in each apple and inserting the worms.
- Create a "shiny apple" award for good behavior or good work.
- Let the students prepare their own open house invitations for their families.

Tab

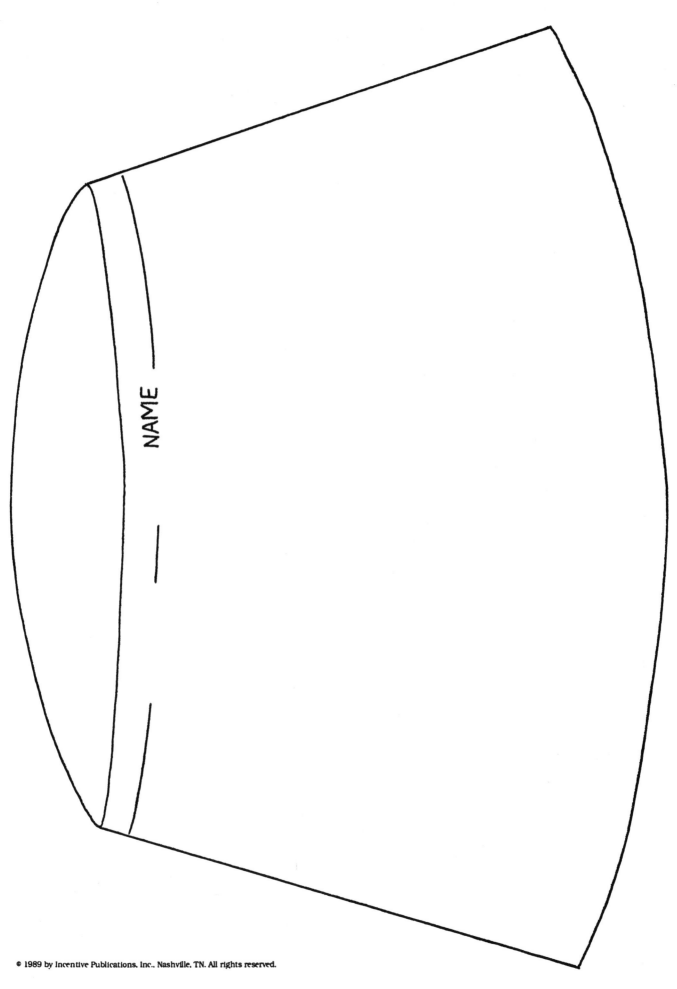

NAME

SUNSHINE SHEET

NAME

Experiment: How clouds are formed.

1. Pour 2 inches of very hot water into a glass jar. Let it stand for a few minutes.
2. Put the jar in a dark spot.
3. Put a metal tray of ice cubes over the top of the jar.
4. Shine a flashlight toward the middle of the jar.
   What happens?   Why?

Construction:
1. Cut the patterns out of construction paper.
2. Prepare the activity or instruct the students to do so.
3. After completing the activity, the students may color the sun and cloud patterns.
4. Instruct each student to fold back the tab and attach the sun to the cloud using glue, paper clips or staples.

Suggestions
Refer to pages 6 - 8 for general subject matter and classroom use suggestions.

- Use sunshine sheets for weather experiment forms and other weather-related activities.
- Attach students' good work to sunshine sheet "backgrounds."
- Create a "Sunshine Award" for good behavior.

Tab

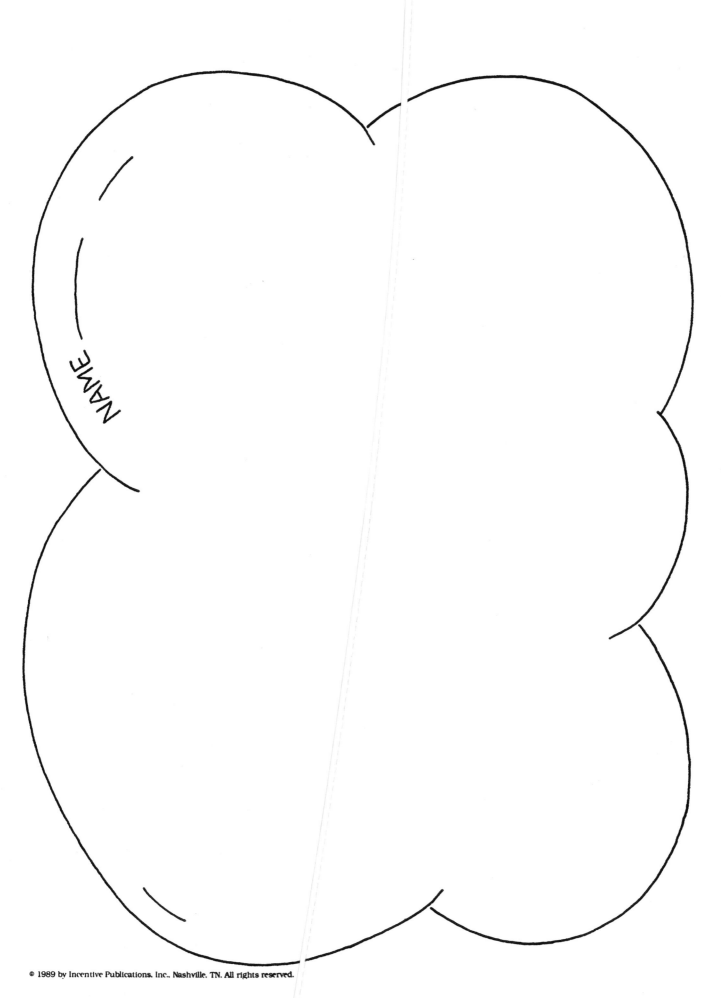

NAME